The

PRAYER
of JABEZ

❧ COURSE WORKBOOK ❧

BRUCE
WILKINSON

Dear friend,

The adventure before you is one more chapter in a spiritual phenomenon. Every day, wherever I may be, I meet people who are discovering the power of God's blessings. Jabez's prayer continues to spark quiet revolutions in the lives of ordinary people like you and me. Has it happened in your life?

I hope so. And even if you've already set out on the Jabez journey, this course will take you deeper into the prayer, wider into the blessings, and farther than ever into expanding your ministry for God. You'll find notes, discussion pages, and features in this workbook to enrich your experience. Are you ready to reach for Jabez blessings?

Yours for blessing and service,

Bruce Wilkinson
President Walk Thru the Bible
Author *The Prayer of Jabez*

Project Director: Dorit Radandt; Design: Randy Drake; Cover Design: Stephen Gardner; Curriculum Development: David Wilkinson; Editor: Rob Suggs; Production: Lois Gable; Cover Photography: Photonica/Tatsuhiko Shimada

TABLE
of CONTENTS

The Structure of This Workbook 4

The Structure of Each Session 5

How to Use This Course 6

Session One: "Bless Me Indeed!"
Part A 7
Part B 13

Session Two: "Enlarge My Territory!"
Part A 19
Part B 25

Special Bible Study Section 31

Session Three: "Put Your Hand on Me!"
Part A 39
Part B 45

Session Four: "Keep Me from Evil!"
Part A 51
Part B 57

THE STRUCTURE
OF
THIS WORKBOOK

The Prayer of Jabez Course Workbook is a companion to the Jabez Video Series and Jabez Seminar. This workbook will enrich your exploration of the Jabez prayer in five ways. Here's how it works:

1 **Introductory Pages:** After the title page and opening comment, you'll find a page geared to build your excitement about the session. Use the quotes for a smile and to jump-start your imagination. Use the self-test to help you think about where you stand with the session topic.

2 **Notes:** Filling in the blanks will help you focus on the key points and insights in this presentation. There's also space to note your own observations.

3 **Group Discussion:** This page offers probing questions about the session topic designed to help you interact with a group. Read each question carefully, reflect on it, and share your ideas with a small group.

4 **Personal Study Pages:** There are six pages for your personal Bible exploration. They introduce the Jabez life, suggest how to live it to the finish line, and dig into each portion of the prayer from the vantage point of other scriptural passages.

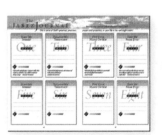

5 **Center Spread:** A colorful journal you can use as a daily reminder to pray the Jabez prayer.

THE STRUCTURE
OF
EACH SESSION

Understand What the Bible Teaches

1 Preview **Study the text** of 1 Chronicles 4:9–10 and the five key Distinctives of each part of the prayer.

2 Pitfalls **Uncover the three** most Common Misconceptions that people have about each part of the prayer and why they are not true.

3 Principles **Become solid** in your understanding of the Jabez Prayer through exploring the three primary biblical truths for each part of the prayer.

Part B: Apply What the Bible Teaches

1 Perspectives **Broaden your understanding** of the major theme of each of the four parts of the Prayer of Jabez through five key perspectives.

2 Practical Steps **Launch immediately** into living the Jabez Life through taking these practical steps for each part of the prayer.

3 Potential **Dream of the potential** for life change that the biblical truths of the Prayer of Jabez could make in your life as you apply them, and start the lifelong habit of the Jabez Life!

HOW TO USE THIS COURSE

1 **Personal Study.** Study *The Prayer of Jabez* at your own pace. Let it transform your personal goals for achievement and impact.

2 **Personal Discipleship.** Study *The Prayer of Jabez* with a friend. Challenge one another to reach for the blessed life.

3 **Family Devotions.** Study *The Prayer of Jabez* as a family. Focus on how God can bless your family and expand its borders.

4 **Small Group.** Study *The Prayer of Jabez* in a home gathering or Bible study class. Watch God bless and minister through your group.

5 **Church Seminar.** Study *The Prayer of Jabez* with your congregation. See God expand your church's influence in the community.

6 **Church Leaders.** Study *The Prayer of Jabez* with deacons or elders. Experience God's hand of power and ministry in a new way.

7 **With Your Company.** Study *The Prayer of Jabez* with your company as an elective meeting before work, during lunch, or after work.

8 **Neighborhood.** Invite your community to experience *The Prayer of Jabez*. Use it to help seekers experience the goodness of God.

BLESS ME INDEED!

What is the first thing that comes to your mind when you think about God? Do you think about His power? His creation? His judgment? How about His love and generosity?

The Bible gives us a clear picture of God's personality. He loves us so deeply that He longs to bless us continually. He yearns to pour out goodness upon us by the week, by the day, by the moment. And that includes you. He wants to bless you right now, as you read these words. Can you imagine the fabulous implications of that?

In this session we'll discover what it means to come to God to ask for the blessings He already longs to give us.

God can't bless you unless you slow down and let Him catch you.
—Anonymous

Dennis the Menace, praying from an airplane: "I been wantin' a horse for a long time—maybe you can hear me better from up here."

WARNING: Frequent intake of God's blessings may cause you to become one yourself.

God sends *showers* of blessing—and I could use a good, long shower about now.

Bless this mess, Lord; there's no messing with Your blessing!

German proverb: If you fold your hands to pray, God will open His to bless.

THE TEST OF THE BLEST

Circle the appropriate number, with 5 indicating "Yes! Absolutely!" and 1 indicating "Never!"

1. I've experienced the Jabez prayer and daily ask God to bless me.

   1   2   3   4   5

2. I'm spotting more and more of God's blessings.

   1   2   3   4   5

3. I think of God as laughing, loving, and lavishing.

   1   2   3   4   5

4. Sometimes God fills me so full that it leaks out on others!

   1   2   3   4   5

5. I bless God more and more for blessing me!

   1   2   3   4   5

SCORING:

5 – 10	Bless This Mess
11 – 15	Less Blessed
16 – 20	Blest-Fest
21 – 25	Blessed Best!

BLESS ME INDEED!

Introduction to the Jabez Prayer

⁹Now Jabez was more honorable than his brothers, and his mother called his name Jabez, saying, "Because I bore him in pain." ¹⁰And Jabez called on the God of Israel saying, "Oh, that You would bless me indeed, and enlarge my territory, that Your hand would be with me, and that You would keep me from evil, that I may not cause pain!" So God granted him what he requested. 1 Chronicles 4:9–10

A "Jabez" means _____

His mother called his name Jabez, saying, "Because I bore him in pain."

B "Honorable" means highly _____

Now Jabez was more honorable than his brothers

¹⁶"Honor your father and your mother, as the LORD your God has commanded you, that your days may be long." Deuteronomy 5:16a

C "Called" means to cry out for _____

Jabez called on the God of Israel saying, "Oh, that You would . . ."

²³Now it happened in the process of time that the king of Egypt died. Then the children of Israel groaned because of the bondage, and they cried out; and their cry came up to God because of the bondage. Exodus 2:23

I. The Preview of the Jabez Blessing

¹⁰And Jabez called on the God of Israel saying, "Oh, that You would bless me indeed!" So God granted him what he requested. 1 Chronicles 4:10

A The Description of the Jabez Blessing

1. "Bless" means to bestow favor or _____

³And his master saw that the LORD was with him and that the LORD made all he did to prosper in his hand. ⁵The LORD blessed the Egyptian's house for Joseph's sake; and the blessing of the LORD was on all that he had in the house and in the field. Genesis 39:3, 5b

2. "Indeed" carries the meaning of greatly or _____

B The Distinctives of the Jabez Blessing

1. The Blessing is not impersonal but _____

2. The Blessing is not specific but _____

Notice a radical aspect of Jabez's request for blessing: He left it entirely up to God to decide what the blessings would be and where, when, and how Jabez would receive them. *The Prayer of Jabez*, page 24.

3. The Blessing is not directed by man but _____

Instead, the Jabez blessing focuses like a laser on our wanting for ourselves nothing more and nothing less than what God wants for us. *The Prayer of Jabez*, page 24.

4. The Blessing is not meager but _____

5. The Blessing is not a weak wish but a fervent _____

II. The Pitfalls of the Jabez Blessing

Misconception #1: *It always works — just say the words!*
The Prayer of Jabez is not _____

Misconception #2: *I can't pray Jabez — it's not right to pray for myself!*
The Prayer of Jabez is not _____

Misconception #3: *If you want to get rich, pray Jabez!*
The Prayer of Jabez is not _____

This kind of radical trust in God's good intentions toward us has nothing in common with the popular gospel that you should ask God for a Cadillac, a six-figure income, or some other material sign that you have found a way to cash in on your connection with Him. *The Prayer of Jabez*, page 24.

> *Our prayers should be for blessings in general,*
> *for God knows best what is good for us.*
> Socrates

III. The Principles of the Jabez Blessing

A The Jabez Blessings are all ultimately from _____

¹⁶*Do not be deceived, my beloved brethren.* ¹⁷*Every good gift and every perfect gift is from above, and comes down from the Father of lights, with whom there is no variation or shadow of turning.*
James 1:16–17

¹¹*"Yours, O LORD, is the greatness, the power and the glory, the victory and the majesty; for all that is in heaven and in earth is Yours; Yours is the kingdom, O LORD, and You are exalted as head over all.* ¹²*Both riches and honor come from You, and You reign over all. In Your hand is power and might; in Your hand it is to make great and to give strength to all."* 1 Chronicles 29:11–12

B The Jabez Blessings are given because God loves to _____

¹⁶*"For God so loved the world that He gave His only begotten Son, that whoever believes in Him should not perish but have everlasting life."* John 3:16

⁶*And the LORD passed before him and proclaimed, "The LORD, the LORD God, merciful and gracious, longsuffering, and abounding in goodness and truth."* Exodus 34:6

⁷*"Thus says the LORD God of Israel: 'I anointed you king over Israel, and I delivered you from the hand of Saul.* ⁸*I gave you your master's house and your master's wives into your keeping, and gave you the house of Israel and Judah. And if that had been too little, I also would have given you much more!'"*
2 Samuel 12:7b–8

C The Jabez Blessings are given to those who _____

⁷*"Ask, and it will be given to you; seek, and you will find; knock, and it will be opened to you.* ⁸*For everyone who asks receives, and he who seeks finds, and to him who knocks it will be opened.* ⁹*Or what man is there among you who, if his son asks for bread, will give him a stone?* ¹⁰*Or if he asks for a fish, will he give him a serpent?* ¹¹*If you then, being evil, know how to give good gifts to your children, how much more will your Father who is in heaven give good things to those who ask Him!"* Matthew 7:7–11

Conclusion

²⁶*And He said, "Let Me go, for the day breaks." But he said, "I will not let You go unless You bless me!"* ²⁹*And He blessed him there.* Genesis 32:26, 29b

1   When you were growing up, who gave you genuine affection and things that brought a sense of blessedness into your life? How many of those things were based upon your relationship with them, and how much upon fulfilling their expectations or requirements?

2   During your lifetime, have you asked God to bless you very often? What would have to happen for you to feel comfortable regularly asking the Lord to pour out His blessing on your life?

3   Did your impression of God match the reality of His mercy, grace, longsuffering, and abounding in goodness? Describe the person you know that is most like those four characteristics. What relationship do you think exists between how a person views God and his freedom to ask Him for blessings?

4   The words in Matthew 7:7–11 are remarkable and downright surprising to many. Read verse 11 and define in your own words these phrases from the passage: "how much more" and "good things" and "those who ask." If you fully embraced that this is the way the Lord works, what would happen in your life?

5   Imagine that you were ushered into the presence of God where He warmly welcomed you and said, "I've been considering major blessings for you. Which one would you like the best?" What would those blessings be, and which one would you select?

BLESS ME INDEED!

God's blessings for you are priceless, profound, and infinite. If you could simply receive all of God's blessings, your life would be changed forever. You would experience all the good things God has intended for you. In time, as you shared your blessings with others, you would become even more blessed yourself.

In this session, we'll discover the variety of God's blessings as the Bible describes them for us. There are many kinds, each one beautiful and unique. Then we'll explore the pattern of living out the blessed life day by day. It's a life of deeper joy and greater abundance. And it's the beginning of the ultimate adventure God has been longing to enjoy with you.

Top Five Blessings in Disguise

1. Yet another day without being smashed by a meteor!

2. Unlike Jabez, no problems with pesky Philistines stealing your cows.

3. Gravity: one law nobody can figure out how to break.

4. God's blessings are never delivered to the wrong address.

5. This list! Reading it kept you from worrying about meteors.

STRANGE BUT TRUE

When the railways were being built across Canada, an American Indian chief named Crowfoot gave permission for trains to cross his territory. The officers gratefully gave him a lifetime railway pass. Crowfoot kept the pass on a chain around his neck for the rest of his life—without ever taking a ride on the train. You have a path to God's blessings. When is the last time you used it?

THE TEST OF THE BLEST

How likely are you to receive blessings from God? Circle the appropriate answers:

1. I experience God's presence frequently and deeply through prayer.

   YES   NO

2. I think of love more than anger when God comes to mind.

   YES   NO

3. I ask God to bless me daily.

   YES   NO

4. I anticipate that God is going to bless me regularly.

   YES   NO

5. I recognize God's blessings frequently.

   YES   NO

SCORING:
Count each yes as 1 point and score yourself this way:

0 – 1	Barely blessed
2	Basically blessed
3	Brightly blessed
4 – 5	Bountifully blessed.

BLESS ME INDEED!

Introduction to the Jabez Prayer

¹⁰And Jabez called on the God of Israel saying, "Oh, that You would bless me indeed, and enlarge my territory, that Your hand would be with me, and that You would keep me from evil, that I may not cause pain!" So God granted him what he requested. 1 Chronicles 4:10

I. The Perspectives on the Jabez Blessing

A The _____ Blessing

Given to everyone freely without any _____

²⁸Then God blessed them, and God said to them, "Be fruitful and multiply; fill the earth and subdue it; have dominion over the fish of the sea, over the birds of the air, and over every living thing that moves on the earth." Genesis 1:28

⁴⁴"But I say to you, love your enemies, bless those who curse you, do good to those who hate you, and pray for those who spitefully use you and persecute you, ⁴⁵that you may be sons of your Father in heaven; for He makes His sun rise on the evil and on the good, and sends rain on the just and on the unjust." Matthew 5:44–45

B The _____ Blessing

Given to those who meet the requirement of _____

¹²"Because you listen to these judgments, and keep and do them, [the] LORD your God will ¹³bless the fruit of your womb and the fruit of your land, your grain and your new wine and your oil, the increase of your cattle and the offspring of your flock." Deuteronomy 7:12b, 13b

⁶"Blessed are those who hunger and thirst for righteousness, for they shall be filled. ⁷Blessed are the merciful, for they shall obtain mercy." Matthew 5:6–7

C The _____ Blessing

Given to those who meet the requirement of _____

⁷"Blessed are those whose lawless deeds are forgiven, and whose sins are covered; ⁸blessed is the man to whom the LORD shall not impute sin." Romans 4:7–8

³Blessed be the God and Father of our Lord Jesus Christ, who has blessed us with every spiritual blessing in the heavenly places in Christ. ⁷In Him we have redemption through His blood, the forgiveness of sins, according to the riches of His grace. Ephesians 1:3, 7

D The _____ Blessing

Given to everyone on the basis of their life, but after _____

¹²*"When you give a dinner or a supper, do not ask your friends, your brothers, your relatives, nor rich neighbors, lest they also invite you back, and you be repaid.* ¹³*But when you give a feast, invite the poor, the maimed, the lame, the blind.* ¹⁴*And you will be blessed, because they cannot repay you; for you shall be repaid at the resurrection of the just."* Luke 14:12–14

¹¹*"Blessed are you when they revile and persecute you, and say all kinds of evil against you falsely for My sake.* ¹²*Rejoice and be exceedingly glad, for great is your reward in heaven, for so they persecuted the prophets who were before you."* Matthew 5:11–12

E The _____ Blessing

Given on the basis of God's character to those who _____

¹*God be merciful to us and bless us.* Psalm 67:1a

II. The Practical Steps for the Jabez Blessing

B _____ **God daily for His bountiful blessings**

¹⁰*And Jabez called on the God of Israel saying, "Oh, that You would bless me indeed!" So God granted him what he requested.* 1 Chronicles 4:10

L _____ **and thank God for His many blessings**

²*Bless the LORD, O my soul, and forget not all His benefits.* Psalm 103:2

E _____ **every blessing that God richly gives you**

¹⁷*Command those who are rich in this present age not to be haughty, nor to trust in uncertain riches but in the living God, who gives us richly all things to enjoy.* 1 Timothy 6:17

S _____ **your blessings with others**

¹⁸*Let them do good, that they be rich in good works, ready to give, willing to share.* 1 Timothy 6:18

S _____ **honor and blessings from God**

⁴¹*"I do not receive honor from men.* ⁴⁴*How can you believe, who receive honor from one another, and do not seek the honor that comes from the only God?"* John 5:41, 44

> *Never undertake anything for which you wouldn't have the courage to ask the blessings of heaven.*
> Georg Christian Lichtenberg

III. The Potential Results from the Jabez Blessing

A **You will** _____ **more of God's blessings**

So God granted him what he requested. 1 Chronicles 4:10c

³"Call to me, and I will answer you, and show you great and mighty things, which you do not know."
Jeremiah 33:3

B **Your heart will be** _____ **by God's blessings**

¹⁷How precious also are Your thoughts to me, O God! How great is the sum of them! ¹⁸If I should count them, they would be more in number than the sand; when I awake, I am still with You.
Psalm 139:17–18

C **Your life will** _____ **blessings to others**

³⁵"I have shown you in every way, by laboring like this, that you must support the weak. And remember the words of the Lord Jesus, that He said, 'It is more blessed to give than to receive.' " Acts 20:35

Conclusion

²²And the LORD spoke to Moses, saying: ²³"Speak to Aaron and his sons, saying, 'This is the way you shall bless the children of Israel. Say to them: ²⁴"The LORD bless you and keep you; ²⁵the LORD make His face shine upon you, and be gracious to you; ²⁶the LORD lift up His countenance upon you, and give you peace." ' " Numbers 6:22–26

INTERACT WITH JABEZ

1 God's desire to bring joy and blessedness to every single person motivated Him in creating the earth and everything therein. Describe the two or three things in creation that bring you the most pleasure.

2 What was the most meaningful blessing that anyone ever gave to you outside of God and your immediate family?

3 Describe the best blessing you ever gave someone else. How did they respond?

4 Sadly, too many of us seem to be better "strivers for" blessings than "enjoyers of" those blessings. Since the Bible says that God gave us richly all things to enjoy, why do you think people often struggle to enjoy the blessings He gives us?

5 If you were shown all the blessings that God intended to give to you in the future if you simply asked Him, what would be your response?

ENLARGE MY TERRITORY!

One thing you're bound to notice about God's blessings: We can't help receiving one without becoming one ourselves. The more God sheds His goodness upon us, the more we find that we overflow into the lives of others. We ask Him for more room, more responsibility, and more range in order to bless the world for Him.

It certainly happened to Jabez. Basking in the blessings, he found himself praying, "God, enlarge my territory." And we know that God did—and He'll do the same for you. Are you ready to take on more, accomplish more, and enjoy more in the service of God?

Top Five Strategies for Enlarging Your Territory

1. Relocate to Antarctica. Own your own continent!

2. Take everyone in the phone book to lunch. Begin with the *A* listings.

3. Find the internet chat room for national presidents. Give them advice.

4. Attend televised sports events. Hold up a huge sign with your phone number.

5. Whenever possible, rescue noted celebrities from burning houses.

STRANGE BUT TRUE

The Japanese carp, or *koi*, grows to two to three inches long in a fishbowl. Placed in a tank or a small pool, however, the same fish may grow to ten inches. In a large pond, it may become eighteen inches. And in a huge lake, the *koi* may reach three feet long! Borders make a difference. Are you a small fish in a big pond?

TERRITORIAL TEST

Are you trapped in a comfort zone? Circle the appropriate answers:

1. I often need new challenges or I tend to grow restless.

    YES   NO

2. I don't run away when God enlarges my territory.

    YES   NO

3. I see a pattern in my life: As I'm faithful, God entrusts me with more territory.

    YES   NO

4. I am praying for expanded responsibilities.

    YES   NO

5. I have a growing desire to do more for God.

    YES   NO

SCORING: Count each yes as 1 point and score yourself this way:

0 – 1	Fenced in
2	Fence-sitter
3	Fence-mover
4 – 5	Fence-buster!

ENLARGE MY TERRITORY!

Introduction to the Jabez Prayer

¹⁰And Jabez called on the God of Israel saying, "Oh, that You would bless me indeed, and enlarge my territory, that Your hand would be with me, and that You would keep me from evil, that I may not cause pain!" So God granted him what he requested. 1 Chronicles 4:10

I. The Preview of the Jabez Territory

¹⁰And Jabez called on the God of Israel saying, "Oh, that You would . . . enlarge my territory!" So God granted him what he requested. 1 Chronicles 4:10

A The Description of the Jabez Territory

1. "Territory" means an area of _____

2. "Border" means the dividing line that _____

3. "Enlarge" means to abundantly _____

   ²²And God blessed them, saying, "Be fruitful and multiply, and fill the waters in the seas, and let birds multiply on the earth." Genesis 1:22

B The Distinctives of the Jabez Territory

Can you imagine a warehouse manager being upset if an employee said, "Sir, I want to do more to make this place really hum for the owner"? Can you imagine a mother being irritated with a child who asks, "What can I do to help you, Mommy?" In the same way, when you ask for greater opportunity for God, He responds with delight and favor. *The Jabez Devotional*, page 35.

1. The Territory is not focused on property but _____

2. The Territory is not focused on money but _____

3. The Territory is not self-initiated but _____

4. The Territory is not focused on comfort but _____

5. The Territory is not limited but _____

II. The Pitfalls of the Jabez Territory

Misconception #1: *God is responsible for the results, not me!*

The Lord will hold you accountable for your life's _____

> [15]"And so it was that when he returned, having received the kingdom, he then commanded these servants, to whom he had given the money, to be called to him, that he might know how much every man had gained by trading. [16]Then came the first, saying, 'Master, your mina has earned ten minas.' [17]And he said to him, 'Well done, good servant; because you were faithful in a very little, have authority over ten cities.' [18]And the second came, saying, 'Master, your mina has earned five minas.' [19]Likewise he said to him, 'You also be over five cities.'" Luke 19:15–19

Misconception #2: *God is interested in spiritual things, not numbers!*

The Lord desires your life to have both quality and _____

> [16]"You did not choose Me, but I chose you and appointed you that you should go and bear fruit, and that your fruit should remain. [8]By this My Father is glorified, that you bear much fruit; so you will be My disciples." John 15:16a, 8

> [41]Then those who gladly received his word were baptized; and that day about three thousand souls were added to them. Acts 2:41

> [4]However, many of those who heard the word believed; and the number of the men came to be about five thousand. Acts 4:4

Misconception #3: *If I'm doing God's will, I won't be afraid!*

The Lord will be with you even when you face _____

> [9]"Have I not commanded you? Be strong and of good courage; do not be afraid, nor be dismayed, for the LORD your God is with you wherever you go." Joshua 1:9

> [5]For He Himself has said, "I will never leave you nor forsake you." [6]So we may boldly say: "The LORD is my helper; I will not fear. What can man do to me?" Hebrews 13:5b–6

> *Behind every work of God you will always find some kneeling form.*
> Dwight L. Moody

III. The Principles of the Jabez Territory

A God will enlarge your territory, but you must break through your _____ _____

¹⁰Then Moses said to the LORD, "O my Lord, I am not eloquent, neither before nor since You have spoken to Your servant; but I am slow of speech and slow of tongue." ¹¹So the LORD said to him, "Who has made man's mouth? Or who makes the mute, the deaf, the seeing, or the blind? Have not I, the Lord? ¹²Now therefore, go, and I will be with your mouth and teach you what you shall say." ¹³But he said, "O my Lord, please send by the hand of whomever else You may send." ¹⁴So the anger of the LORD was kindled against Moses.   Exodus 4:10–14a

B God will enlarge your territory, but you must overcome your _____ _____

³²"The land through which we have gone as spies is a land that devours its inhabitants, and all the people whom we saw in it are men of great stature. ³³There we saw the giants (the descendants of Anak came from the giants); and we were like grasshoppers in our own sight, and so we were in their sight." ⁹"Only do not rebel against the LORD, nor fear the people of the land, for they are our bread; their protection has departed from them, and the LORD is with us. Do not fear them."   Numbers 13:32b–33; 14:9

C God will enlarge your territory, but you must struggle to _____ _____

³⁰"The LORD your God, who goes before you, He will fight for you, according to all He did for you in Egypt before your eyes. ⁴¹"We will go up and fight, just as the LORD our God commanded us.' And when everyone of you had girded on his weapons of war, you were ready to go up into the mountain."   Deuteronomy 1:30, 41b

¹¹"Pass through the camp and command the people, saying, 'Prepare provisions for yourselves, for within three days you will cross over this Jordan, to go in to possess the land which the LORD your God is giving you to possess.'"   Joshua 1:11

Conclusion

³³And Saul said to David, "You are not able to go against this Philistine to fight with him; for you are a youth, and he a man of war from his youth." ³⁴But David said to Saul, ³⁶"Your servant has killed both lion and bear; and this uncircumcised Philistine will be like one of them, seeing he has defied the armies of the living God." ³⁷Moreover David said, "The LORD, who delivered me from the paw of the lion and from the paw of the bear, He will deliver me from the hand of this Philistine." And Saul said to David, "Go, and the LORD be with you!"   1 Samuel 17:33–34a, 36–37

1. Take a piece of paper and draw a circle representing your current territory. Inside of those "borders" write the *what* and *who* God may include in your territory.

2. Many people are afraid to pray the Jabez prayer because of fear that God may answer it and enlarge their territory! What fears would cause them to feel that way, and how could they be defeated?

3. Have you ever experienced God enlarging your territory—even before you started praying the Jabez prayer? What happened?

4. When you think about your life, what areas do you think have been the most productive for the Lord? How could you maximize them even further?

5. Close your eyes and picture the "border bullies" standing at the edges of your "comfort zone." Who are they and how could you conquer them?

ENLARGE MY TERRITORY!

What are the borders that define your life? We all have our limits, don't we? We're limited by the people we know, the places we go, and the work we accomplish. But isn't it time we let ourselves be defined by opportunity rather than limitation?

God is calling you to a new life that boldly ventures outside those places where you feel comfortable and unchallenged. He knows you'll never feel genuinely alive unless you go where the action is. He wants to expand your circles of influence and impact. In this session we'll discover what life looks like beyond the comfort zone, in the place where natural limitations give way to supernatural power.

Lord, grant that I may always desire more than I can accomplish.
—*Michelangelo*

Christianity is not believing the impossible, but doing the incredible.
—*Sherwood Eddy*

Aim at heaven and you get earth thrown in; aim at earth and you get neither.
—*C. S. Lewis*

Shoot for the moon. Even if you miss it, you will land among the stars.
—*Les Brown*

Aim at nothing and you'll succeed.
—*Anonymous*

ARE YOU A BORDER-BUSTER?

Circle the right number, with 5 indicating "Yes! Absolutely!" and 1 indicating "Never!"

1. I have felt a restlessness to take on greater challenges.

   1   2   3   4   5

2. I have often asked God to enlarge my territory.

   1   2   3   4   5

3. I have a growing clarity of where God is enlarging my territory.

   1   2   3   4   5

4. I'm rearranging my priorities to move into new territory.

   1   2   3   4   5

5. I am willing to take on greater challenges.

   1   2   3   4   5

SCORING:

5 – 10	Planted
11 – 15	Pace-setter
16 – 20	Pilgrim
21 – 25	Pioneer!

ENLARGE MY TERRITORY!

Introduction to the Jabez Prayer

[10]And Jabez called on the God of Israel saying, "Oh, that You would bless me indeed, and enlarge my territory, that Your hand would be with me, and that You would keep me from evil, that I may not cause pain!" So God granted him what he requested. 1 Chronicles 4:10

I. The Perspectives on the Jabez Territory

[18]And Jesus came and spoke to them, saying, "All authority has been given to Me in heaven and on earth. [19]Go therefore and make disciples of all the nations, baptizing them in the name of the Father and of the Son and of the Holy Spirit, [20]teaching them to observe all things that I have commanded you; and lo, I am with you always, even to the end of the age." Amen. Matthew 28:18–20

A God enlarges your territory by increasing its _____

God enables you to serve Him by doing more of the _____

[8]"But you shall receive power when the Holy Spirit has come upon you; and you shall be witnesses to Me in Jerusalem, and in all Judea and Samaria, and to the end of the earth." Acts 1:8

B God enlarges your territory by extending its _____

God enables you to serve Him by doing something _____

[18]And Jesus, walking by the Sea of Galilee, saw two brothers, Simon called Peter, and Andrew his brother, casting a net into the sea; for they were fishermen. [19]Then He said to them, "Follow Me, and I will make you fishers of men." [20]They immediately left their nets and followed Him. Matthew 4:18–20

C God enlarges your territory by sharpening your _____

God enables you to serve Him by doing something _____

[17]As for these four young men, God gave them knowledge and skill in all literature and wisdom. [19]Then the king interviewed them, and among them all none was found like Daniel, Hananiah, Mishael, and Azariah; therefore they served before the king. [20]And in all matters of wisdom and understanding about which the king examined them, he found them ten times better than all the magicians and astrologers who were in all his realm. Daniel 1:17a, 19–20

D God enlarges your territory by improving your _____

God enables you to serve Him by doing something more _____

¹⁷So Moses' father-in-law said to him, "The thing that you do is not good. ¹⁸Both you and these people who are with you will surely wear yourselves out. For this thing is too much for you; you are not able to perform it by yourself. ²¹Moreover you shall select from all the people able men, such as fear God, men of truth, hating covetousness; and place such over them to be rulers of thousands, rulers of hundreds, rulers of fifties, and rulers of tens. ²²And let them judge the people at all times. Then it will be that every great matter they shall bring to you, but every small matter they themselves shall judge. So it will be easier for you, for they will bear the burden with you." Exodus 18:17–18, 21–22

E God enlarges your territory by deepening its _____

God enables you to serve Him by doing something more _____

¹⁴Then Pharaoh sent and called Joseph, and they brought him quickly out of the dungeon; and he shaved, changed his clothing, and came to Pharaoh. ³⁹Then Pharaoh said to Joseph, "Inasmuch as God has shown you all this, there is no one as discerning and wise as you. ⁴⁰You shall be over my house, and all my people shall be ruled according to your word; only in regard to the throne will I be greater than you." Genesis 41:14, 39–40

II. The Practical Steps for the Jabez Territory

E _____ **your territory by earnestly praying the Jabez Prayer**

N _____ **your family of your Jabez commitment**

L _____ **to recognize a Jabez moment**

A _____ **ministry opportunities that stretch your faith**

R _____ **your time, talents, and treasure**

G _____ **God by crediting Him openly**

E _____ **your territory through the final season of life**

¹⁰"Now, here I am this day, eighty-five years old. ¹²Now therefore, give me this mountain of which the LORD spoke in that day; for you heard in that day how the Anakim [giants] were there, and that the cities were great and fortified. It may be that the LORD will be with me, and I shall be able to drive them out as the LORD said." Joshua 14:10c, 12

> *God does not begin by asking us about our ability, but only about our availability, and if we then prove our dependability, He will increase our capability!*
> Neal A. Maxwell

III. The Potential Results from the Jabez Territory

A You will _____ a miraculous partnership with God

[19]Or do you not know that your body is the temple of the Holy Spirit who is in you, whom you have from God, and you are not your own? [20]For you were bought at a price; therefore glorify God in your body and in your spirit, which are God's. 1 Corinthians 6:19–20

[8]For by grace you have been saved through faith, and that not of yourselves; it is the gift of God, [9]not of works, lest anyone should boast. [10]For we are His workmanship, created in Christ Jesus for good works, which God prepared beforehand that we should walk in them. Ephesians 2:8–10

B You will do great _____ for God in your generation

[32]But the people who know their God shall be strong, and carry out great exploits. [33]And those of the people who understand shall instruct many. Daniel 11:32b–33a

C You will _____ the Lord's "Well done!"

[21]"His lord said to him, 'Well done, good and faithful servant; you were faithful over a few things, I will make you ruler over many things. Enter into the joy of your lord.'" Matthew 25:21

Conclusion

[9]After these things I looked, and behold, a great multitude which no one could number, of all nations, tribes, peoples, and tongues, standing before the throne and before the Lamb, clothed with white robes, with palm branches in their hands, [10]and crying out with a loud voice, saying, "Salvation belongs to our God who sits on the throne, and to the Lamb!" Revelation 7:9–10

INTERACT WITH JABEZ

1 If the Lord were to maximize your life through increasing the size of your territory, what do you think He would do?

2 Identify one talent or gift that may have slid to the "neglected and unused" box. If you brought it out, brushed it off, and then used it to serve God this next month, how could you use it?

3 What is one area in your life that you can't seem to break through in serving the Lord? Think of new strategies to enlarge your territory that you could try in the next few weeks.

4 List the top responsibilities in your life. Which two accomplish the most for the Lord and His Kingdom? What could you do to double their productivity?

5 If you could do only one "great exploit" for God in your life from this point forward, what would be the first step to make it happen?

The Jabez Life

READ HEBREWS 11

Who can do the impossible with God's help? A lot of people, according to Hebrews 11! Here's a parade of ordinary men and women who were extraordinary achievers. The world says, "Seeing is believing," but for the faithful, "Believing is seeing." Here are some who believed.

The first verse defines faith as "the substance of things hoped for, the evidence of things not seen." That means faith is concerned with the future and the invisible. It transforms tomorrow's potential into today's reality; it gives substance to the invisible and undoable. It's Jabez faith.

This chapter is a collection of the "border-busters." God blessed them, and they responded by stepping out in faith toward great achievements. And the point isn't that these people are heroes, but that they're just like us. If they lived the Jabez life, why can't you? Read the case studies and reflect on these questions:

1   How would you explain to a friend, in your own words, the definition of faith in verse 1?

2   Who is your favorite champion of faith in this chapter? How did this person expand his or her territory?

3   How did faith define these people's lives? How did they use it to reach for God's blessings?

4   Hebrews 11:3 tells us that this is a visible world, created and ruled by an invisible God. How does this truth connect with your desire to seek God's blessing and achieve more for Him?

5   Read Hebrews 12:1. What "weights" and sins should you set aside? How will you move forward in faith?

The
JABEZ JOURNAL

Get a sense of God's presence, provision,

BLESS ME INDEED!

WEEK *One*

"I live in the spirit of prayer; I pray as I walk, when I lie down, and when I rise, and the answers are always coming." GEORGE MUELLER

ENLARGE MY TERRITORY!

WEEK *Two*

"Prayer is the key that opens to us the treasures of God's mercies and blessings."
AUTHOR UNKNOWN

BLESS ME INDEED!

WEEK *Five*

ENLARGE MY TERRITORY!

WEEK *Six*

Record one special "Jabez Moment" each week.

power and protection, in your life in the next eight weeks!

PUT YOUR HAND ON ME!

Three

WEEK

"The hand of God never deals but in concert with His heart of infinite love toward us."
JOHN DARBY

KEEP ME FROM EVIL!

Four

WEEK

"Jesus is more ready to pardon than you are to sin, more willing to supply your wants than you are to confess them." CHARLES SPURGEON

PUT YOUR HAND ON ME!

Seven

WEEK

KEEP ME FROM EVIL!

Eight

WEEK

Jabez Blessings

READ EPHESIANS 1:3–14

Ephesians 1:3–14 is a full inventory of your wonderful legacy in Christ. You might call it the contents of your spiritual blessings box.

"Blessed be the God and Father . . . who has blessed us" (v. 3). We bless and praise God because He has blessed us "with every spiritual blessing in the heavenly places in Christ" (v. 30). So it's a two-way blessing. As you read on, you'll discover blessings from your past (why God made you), your present (where you stand in Christ, vv. 5–6), and your future (coming into your inheritance, v. 14).

Then there are overflowing blessings, listed in verses 7–14: redemption and forgiveness (v. 7); wisdom and prudence (understanding) (v. 8); knowing His will (v. 9); an inheritance (v. 11). How do we use these blessings? We're told twice: "to the praise of His glory" (vv. 12, 14).

1 How can blessings be in the heavenly places?

2 How can you practice the two-way blessing in Ephesians 1:3 (receiving His blessings and giving some back)? Which blessings in verses 7–14 are most meaningful to you? Why?

3 How have you experienced each of the blessing you noted above? Which have you understood the least?

4 What is meant by "to the praise of His glory"? How can you do that?

5 These are primarily *spiritual* blessings. How do they affect your life in the *natural* world?

Jabez Borders

READ DEUTERONOMY 1:6–8

How did eleven days become thirty-eight years? Moses despaired over that question. The Israelites had been on an eleven-day march from the Promised Land that God had prepared for them. Instead they wandered for thirty-eight years—the price of refusing to trust God for victory.

"See, I have set the land before you," God said. "Go in and possess the land which the Lord swore to your fathers" (Deuteronomy 1:8a). Just on the brink of the prize, with glory in their grasp, God's people failed to reach out and take the blessing for their own.

God's rebuke is haunting: "You have dwelt long enough at this mountain. Turn and take your journey, and go to the mountains of the Amorites" (vv. 6b–7a). Have you ever clung to the old mountain much too long? As you study these three verses, ponder these questions:

1 The Israelites had shrunk back for fear of giants in the land. What "giants" cause you to shrink back from the blessings God has promised?

2 What factors (other than fear) make us hesitate to enlarge our territory?

3 God sets the "land" before us (v. 8). If that became our mindset, how would it affect our attitudes about taking on greater things for Him?

4 What old "mountain" are you clinging to? What new one is God beckoning you to?

5 What steps will you take as you ask God to extend your boundaries into your own land of promise?

Jabez Power

READ JOHN 14:12–18

Of all the promises Jesus ever made, this may be the most startling: "Most assuredly . . . he who believes in Me, the works that I do he will do also; and greater works than these he will do" (John 14:12). Did we hear that right?

Yes! Jesus underlined it with "most assuredly," then explained it in Acts 1:8: We work with the same power but with wider impact. We go places where the feet of Jesus never trod. We take greater territory and impact more people. We see miracles today—beyond yesterday's borders.

Jesus lays out the plan for us in this passage: *1. Believe; 2. Ask; 3. Obey.* Then you'll draw on an incredible power the world can never understand. And you'll go, with Jesus, where no one has gone before.

1 How does the process of *believe, ask,* and *obey* involve us with the work of God in this world? How does it happen in your life?

2 What is the key to asking from God, according to vv. 13–14? What will be the result?

3 What does keeping His commandments (v. 15) have to do with working in God's power?

4 The word "Spirit" (v. 16) means *Helper* or *Comforter.* How will these two attributes affect your work for God?

5 Jesus promises He'll never leave us as orphans, but that He'll come to us (v. 18). How should this idea give you even greater power? How will this idea change the way you work?

Jabez Protection

READ 1 CORINTHIANS 10:12–13

Beware! That's what Paul is trying to say. *Take care lest you take a plunge!* When you serve God, you're living and serving on a higher plane, and it's a long way to the bottom. One false step will undo a lot of climbing. Also, a "little" sin on your part will affect many people. So beware—great service attracts great temptation.

That's why it's so comforting to have the promises we find in these two short verses. While temptation can be strong, God is always stronger. We know that anything we face is "common to man" (another translation would be, "no more than human"). And God has set a ceiling on how much we endure. We're promised that we'll never be tempted beyond our natural capacity and He will always provide an escape hatch. Fair enough!

1 Why can it be so easy to stumble into sin when we're serving God? Why aren't we immune?

2 What point is Paul making by assuring us that these particular temptations aren't new? How can you use that to gain strength for protection?

3 How can God's faithfulness make a difference when you're undergoing temptation?

4 God makes *the* way (that is, one particular way) of escape for every temptation. How do you think that escape can be found?

5 What is your weak point in regard to temptation? How can you protect yourself so you don't stumble?

The Jabez Finish Line!

READ PHILIPPIANS 3:12–14

There he sat in a dark, damp prison cell, with a poster on the wall reading, "Today is the first day of the rest of your life!" Maybe not, but it would be typical of Paul's infectious faith and optimism. He had no liberty of movement, but his heart was free as a bird. He was locked in, yet he spoke of sprinting toward the horizon, extending his boundaries to the world itself.

Paul lived in joy because his eyes were set on the finish line: taking the gospel throughout the empire. He strained forward for tomorrow with no regard for yesterday. Paul cared about nothing but seizing the one thing for which Jesus had seized him. That's the Jabez life, and it's all about the pursuit of a worthy prize. What will you pursue?

1 How would you explain in your own words the central message of Paul's verses?

2 Paul says "one thing" he does. How important is it to be focused? How can you attain that focus?

3 What do you believe to be the goal for which God has taken hold of you? Why?

4 How can you be better at "forgetting those things which are behind"?

5 How will you begin today to make the "upward call" the center of your pursuit?

PUT YOUR HAND ON ME!

I t's time to talk about power, a kind of power few people ever experience. All the things we think of as "powerful" are nothing when compared to the hand that formed the universe. It's the same hand that wants to rest upon you and me.

God's Hand is often experienced beyond our comfort zones. It comes when we feel overwhelmed. We experience it when we reach for new territory and seek to do something significant for God, out of a heart of obedience. God wants to empower you for awesome ministry. Are you ready for it?

I'm caught in a power struggle. God has the power, and I have the struggle.
—*Anonymous*

When I pray, coincidences happen. When I don't, they don't.
—*William Temple*

Without God's power, you're an empty glove. You need to be filled with a powerful hand to do what you were meant to accomplish.
—*Corrie ten Boom*

We are all faced with innumerable opportunities brilliantly disguised as impossible situations.
—*Chuck Swindoll*

Our prayers lay the track down on which God's power can come. Like a mighty locomotive, his power is irresistible, but it cannot reach us without rails.
—*Watchman Nee*

WHAT'S YOUR POWER RATING?

Circle the right number, with 5 indicating "Yes! Absolutely!" and 1 indicating "Never!"

1. I have taken on challenges that simply overwhelmed me.

   1   2   3   4   5

2. I have found myself feeling inadequate to achieve my goals.

   1   2   3   4   5

3. I truly yearn to feel the power of God moving through my life.

   1   2   3   4   5

4. I'm willing to face my weaknesses to know His sufficiency.

   1   2   3   4   5

5. I'm willing to take on an impossible challenge today.

   1   2   3   4   5

SCORING:

5 – 10	Flower power
11 – 15	Will power
16 – 20	Super power
21 – 25	Nuclear power

PUT YOUR HAND ON ME!

Introduction to the Jabez Prayer

10And Jabez called on the God of Israel saying, "Oh, that You would bless me indeed, and enlarge my territory, that Your hand would be with me, and that You would keep me from evil, that I may not cause pain!" So God granted him what he requested. 1 Chronicles 4:10

I. The Preview of the Jabez "Hand of God"

10And Jabez called on the God of Israel saying, "Oh, that Your hand would be with me!" So God granted him what he requested. 1 Chronicles 4:10

A The Description of the Jabez "Hand of God"

1. "Hand of God" carries the meaning of God's _____

2. "Would be with me" asks God to act on his _____

B The Distinctives of the Jabez "Hand of God"

Imagine that you're climbing a mountain for the first time, and you've stopped on a dangerous ledge. Your hands and legs begin to tremble uncontrollably. You can't move forward or backward, and you don't know what to do. Then your guide (an older, much more experienced mountaineer) reaches out and grips your hand. He looks you in the eyes and says, "It's okay. I've got you. Just move forward . . . slowly . . . move one foot . . . now the other." Clinging to his hand, you inch your way across the ledge until you finally reach solid ground. Without his help, you never would have made it. It's like that with God's helping hand. *The Prayer of Jabez for Kids*, pages 53–54.

1. The "Hand of God" is not merely God's power but God's _____

2. The "Hand of God" is not human ingenuity but divine _____

3. The "Hand of God" is not natural but _____

4. The "Hand of God" is not for my wishes but His _____

5. The "Hand of God" is not subjective feelings but objective _____

II. The Pitfalls regarding the Jabez "Hand of God"

Misconception #1: *Only people in the Bible experienced the "Hand of God."*
The "Hand of God" is available anytime to _____

¹³Gideon said to Him, "O my lord, if the LORD is with us, why then has all this happened to us? And where are all His miracles which our fathers told us about, saying, 'Did not the LORD bring us up from Egypt?' But now the LORD has forsaken us and delivered us into the hands of the Midianites."
Judges 6:13

Misconception #2: *You must surrender control to see the "Hand of God."*
The "Hand of God" requires you to control your body and _____

²²But the fruit of the Spirit is love, joy, peace, longsuffering, kindness, goodness, faithfulness, ²³gentleness, self-control. Galatians 5:22–23a

⁵Bringing every thought into captivity to the obedience of Christ. 2 Corinthians 10:5b

Misconception #3: *You gain spiritual power the more God uses you.*
The "Hand of God" nor your godliness gives you personal _____

¹²So when Peter saw it, he responded to the people: "Men of Israel, why do you marvel at this? Or why look so intently at us, as though by our own power or godliness we had made this man walk? ¹⁶And His name, through faith in His name, has made this man strong, whom you see and know. Yes, the faith which comes through Him has given him this perfect soundness in the presence of you all." Acts 3:12, 16

¹²Then all the multitude kept silent and listened to Barnabas and Paul declaring how many miracles and wonders God had worked through them among the Gentiles. Acts 15:12

> *God has called us to live a life we cannot live, so that we must depend on Him for supernatural ability. We are called to do the impossible, to live beyond our natural ability.*
> Erwin W. Lutzer

III. The Principles of the Jabez "Hand of God"

A The "Hand of God" is the requirement of God for the work of _____

⁴⁹"Behold, I send the Promise of My Father upon you; but tarry in the city of Jerusalem until you are endued with power from on high." Luke 24:49

⁸"But you shall receive power when the Holy Spirit has come upon you; and you shall be witnesses to Me in Jerusalem, and in all Judea and Samaria, and to the end of the earth." Acts 1:8

²¹And the hand of the Lord was with them, and a great number believed and turned to the Lord. Acts 11:21

B The "Hand of God" is hindered by the sin of _____

⁵⁷So they were offended at Him. But Jesus said to them, "A prophet is not without honor except in his own country and in his own house." ⁵⁸Now He did not do many mighty works there because of their unbelief. Matthew 13:57–58

¹⁹Then the disciples came to Jesus privately and said, "Why could we not cast it out?" ²⁰So Jesus said to them, "Because of your unbelief; for assuredly, I say to you, if you have faith as a mustard seed, you will say to this mountain, 'Move from here to there,' and it will move; and nothing will be impossible for you." Matthew 17:19–20

C The "Hand of God" should be experienced in your _____

²⁸Him we preach, warning every man and teaching every man in all wisdom, that we may present every man perfect in Christ Jesus. ²⁹To this end I also labor, striving according to His working which works in me mightily. Colossians 1:28–29

Conclusion

⁹"For the eyes of the LORD run to and fro throughout the whole earth, to show Himself strong on behalf of those whose heart is loyal to Him." 2 Chronicles 16:9a

INTERACT WITH JABEZ

1 Of all the people you have known throughout your life, which one would you say has the "Hand of God" the most? What made you select that person?

2 Why do you think some people believe that a sign of God's Hand or power coming over them is the loss of control? When God did miracles in the Old Testament and New Testament, did any of the people lose control?

3 Unbelief is a serious sin in the Bible. Read Numbers 14:11–12 and 20–23 and describe the Lord's attitude about the nation's unbelief. How many times did the Lord miraculously intervene on behalf of Israel before He moved in judgment? What can you learn about God from this?

4 As God searches "to and fro throughout the earth," do you think He finds many "whose heart is loyal to Him"? List as many differences as you can between a person who is loyal and a person who is disloyal to God.

5 Describe the time in your life when you experienced the movement of the "Hand of God" the most vividly. How would you describe the situation before and after God showed up?

PUT YOUR HAND ON ME!

*Y*ou've heard about it for so long. You've seen it in God's Word. And if you've been in the right places, you've seen evidence of it in others. We're talking about the supernatural power of God. Wouldn't you like to experience it yourself? Don't you feel it's time to stop hearing about it and start living it?

God's power isn't monopolized by the "spiritual elite." It was never limited to just people who lived in biblical times. God's power is for here, for now, and for you. In this session you'll learn more about God's power for God's purposes. You'll be amazed at what your life will look like when you live and walk the incredible journey of the Jabez Adventure.

Top Five Overwhelming, Jabez-Sized Goals for Those Who Think Big

1. You take your message to the exact opposite side of the world—using a shovel.

2. "The world" isn't a big enough goal, so you add the Milky Way galaxy.

3. Not content merely to walk on water, you try it on roller skates while juggling.

4. Your mission statement glows in the dark and can be read from the space shuttle.

5. You decide to bring America and Europe together. You plan to use duct tape.

STRANGE BUT TRUE

George Mueller opened a children's home and depended solely on God to handle its every need. Once there was no food for the children's breakfast, and a meat truck broke down just outside. The driver provided the meal. These miracles were common occurrences, and Mueller logged ten thousand answered prayers during his career!

PRIMED FOR POWER

Will God send His power upon you? Test yourself. Circle the appropriate answers:

1. I tend to rely on my own skills and personality when faced with a challenge.

   TRUE   FALSE

2. I'm more of a doer than a thinker, so I'm often too busy for prayer.

   TRUE   FALSE

3. I tend to remain in a "safe" situation rather than take a risk of failing.

   TRUE   FALSE

4. When overwhelmed, I retreat to a more comfortable setting.

   TRUE   FALSE

5. I don't see myself as having a ministry; maybe I'll be ready someday.

   TRUE   FALSE

SCORING: Count each TRUE as 1 point and score yourself this way:

0 – 1	Turned off
2	Plugged in
3	Charged up
4 – 5	Power packed!

PUT YOUR HAND ON ME!

Introduction to the Jabez Prayer

¹⁰And Jabez called on the God of Israel saying, "Oh, that You would bless me indeed, and enlarge my territory, that Your hand would be with me, and that You would keep me from evil, that I may not cause pain!" So God granted him what he requested. 1 Chronicles 4:10

I. The Perspectives on the Jabez "Hand of God"

A The "Hand of God" intervenes to make _____

God can provide the needed personal and ministry _____

²¹And Moses said, "The people whom I am among are six hundred thousand men on foot; yet You have said, 'I will give them meat, that they may eat for a whole month.' ²²Shall flocks and herds be slaughtered for them, to provide enough for them? Or shall all the fish of the sea be gathered together for them, to provide enough for them?" ²³And the LORD said to Moses, "Has the LORD's arm been shortened? Now you shall see whether what I say will happen to you or not." Numbers 11:21–23

³¹"Therefore do not worry, saying, 'What shall we eat?' or 'What shall we drink?' or 'What shall we wear?' ³²For after all these things the Gentiles seek. For your heavenly Father knows that you need all these things. ³³But seek first the kingdom of God and His righteousness, and all these things shall be added to you." Matthew 6:31–33

¹⁹And my God shall supply all your need according to His riches in glory by Christ Jesus. Philippians 4:19

B The "Hand of God" intervenes to cause an authority to grant _____

God can make your authority change his mind and grant your _____

The king's heart is in the hand of the LORD, like the rivers of water; He turns it wherever He wishes. Proverbs 21:1

⁷Furthermore I said to the king, "If it pleases the king, let letters be given to me for the governors of the region beyond the River, that they must permit me to pass through till I come to Judah, ⁸and a letter to Asaph the keeper of the king's forest, that he must give me timber to make beams for the gates of the citadel which pertains to the temple, for the city wall, and for the house that I will occupy." And the king granted them to me according to the good hand of my God upon me. Nehemiah 2:7–8

C The "Hand of God" intervenes with His _____

God can make His presence known in a specific _____

[16]*So he answered, "Do not fear, for those who are with us are more than those who are with them."* [17]*And Elisha prayed, and said, "LORD, I pray, open his eyes that he may see." Then the LORD opened the eyes of the young man, and he saw. And behold, the mountain was full of horses and chariots of fire all around Elisha.* 2 Kings 6:16–17

[15]*Then he said to Him, "If Your Presence does not go with us, do not bring us up from here.* [16]*For how then will it be know that Your people and I have found grace in Your sight, except You go with us?"* Exodus 33:15-16a

D The "Hand of God" intervenes to defend and _____

God can protect you from any human or spiritual _____

[10]*"Then Pilate said to Him, "Are You not speaking to me? Do You not know that I have power to crucify You, and power to release You?"* [11]*Jesus answered, "You could have no power at all against Me unless it had been given you from above. Therefore the one who delivered Me to you has the greater sin."* John 19:10–11

[17]*"If that is the case, our God whom we serve is able to deliver us from the burning fiery furnace, and He will deliver us from your hand, O king.* [18]*But if not, let it be known to you, O king, that we do not serve your gods, nor will we worship the gold image which you have set up."* Daniel 3:17–18

[10]*Finally, my brethren, be strong in the Lord and in the power of His might.* [11]*Put on the whole armor of God, that you may be able to stand against the wiles of the devil.* Ephesians 6:10–11

E The "Hand of God" intervenes to overcome limitations with His _____

God is not limited by any of your inadequacies or _____

[9]*And He said to me, "My grace is sufficient for you, for My strength is made perfect in weakness." Therefore most gladly I will rather boast in my infirmities, that the power of Christ may rest upon me.* [10]*Therefore I take pleasure in infirmities, in reproaches, in needs, in persecutions, in distresses, for Christ's sake. For when I am weak, then I am strong.* 2 Corinthians 12:9–10

[13]*I can do all things through Christ who strengthens me.* Philippians 4:13

> *The Christian life is stamped all through with impossibility. Human nature cannot come anywhere near what Jesus Christ demands, and any rational being facing His demands honestly, says, "It can't be done, apart from a miracle." Exactly.*
>
> Oswald Chambers

II. The Practical Steps for the Jabez "Hand of God"

H_____ yourself under the mighty "Hand of God"

⁶Therefore humble yourselves under the mighty hand of God, that He may exalt you in due time. 1 Peter 5:6

A_____ a lifestyle of proactive dependency upon God

⁴"Abide in Me, and I in you. As the branch cannot bear fruit of itself, unless it abides in the vine, neither can you, unless you abide in Me. ⁵I am the vine, you are the branches. He who abides in Me, and I in him, bears much fruit; for without Me you can do nothing." John 15:4–5

N_____ your focus to what God wants done

³³"But seek first the kingdom of God and His righteousness, and all these things shall be added to you." Matthew 6:33

D_____ yourself to live an ever increasing walk of faith

¹⁶[I] do not cease to give thanks for you, making mention of you in my prayers: [so you will know] ¹⁹what is the exceeding greatness of His power toward us who believe, according to the working of His mighty power ²⁰which He worked in Christ when He raised Him from the dead and seated Him at His right hand in the heavenly places. Ephesians 1:16, 19–20

²⁰Now to Him who is able to do exceedingly abundantly above all that we ask or think, according to the power that works in us. Ephesians 3:20

III. The Potential Results from the Jabez "Hand of God"

A You will see the "Hand of God" miraculously _____

B You will see the "Hand of God" move beyond your _____

C You will see the "Hand of God" overcome the _____

Conclusion

⁶"This is the word of the LORD to Zerubbabel: 'Not by might nor by power, but by My Spirit,' says the LORD of hosts." Zechariah 4:6

INTERACT WITH JABEZ

1 Have you ever taken such a bold step of faith in ministry for God that you were completely dependent on God's power? What happened? How do you think Joshua felt when God instructed him to walk around Jericho seven times and shout to make the walls fall down (Joshua 6:1–20)?

2 A fine line exists between faith and presumption, between properly trusting in God and impetuously presuming that God will come through for you. How would you describe the difference? For a couple of interesting illustrations of presumption, read Numbers 14:39–45 and Esther 7:5–10.

3 Why did the Lord repeatedly encourage Moses and Joshua that He would be with them? How does the Lord's presence dispel fear? In the great commission, why do you think Jesus reminded the disciples, "I am with you always, even to the end of the age" (Matthew 28:18-20)?

4 Faith is a muscle that grows stronger or weaker depending on use. List some ways that the Lord stretched your faith in your lifetime.

5 Many people won't step out in faith because of fear of criticism or fear of making a mistake. After all, how can one be sure when walking by faith, not sight?

KEEP ME FROM EVIL!

W e've spoken of the lavish blessings of God. We've described the adventure of taking on more for Him. And we've experienced the awesome power that He makes available for such a life. Have we left something out? Yes, there's one more thing. As your territory expands you need to understand how God keeps you from evil.

Just as you start experiencing God's power, that's when even greater temptations may come to distract you from the great work at hand. In this session we'll discover how to pray and stand firm in the face of temptation.

Temptation creeps in through doors we've been reluctant to lock.

Temptations are tramps: Treat them kindly and they return with their friends.
—*The Link*

Most people who fly from temptation usually leave a forwarding address.
—*Anonymous*

Adversity causes some men to break, others to break records.
—*William A. Ward*

If temptation tries to change your direction—turn to the *right* until it has *left!*

THINK ABOUT IT

When a hawk is attacked by crows, he never counterattacks. Instead, he soars higher and higher in ever widening circles until his tormentors leave him alone.

WHERE'S THE CHINK IN YOUR ARMOR?

Place a 1 beside your greatest weak spot. Place a 2 beside the next worst, and so on. Use this list for daily prayer for protection from evil.

__ Materialism

__ Pride

__ Self-Centeredness

__ Laziness

__ Anger and Bitterness

__ Sexual lust

__ Envy

__ Gluttony

__ Lying

__ Other: _____

Name of a friend with whom you can share this list for prayer support:

_____

KEEP ME FROM EVIL!

Introduction to the Jabez Prayer

[10]And Jabez called on the God of Israel saying, "Oh, that You would bless me indeed, and enlarge my territory, that Your hand would be with me, and that You would keep me from evil, that I may not cause pain!" So God granted him what he requested. 1 Chronicles 4:10

I. The Preview of the Jabez "Keep Me from Evil"

[10]And Jabez called on the God of Israel saying, "Oh, that You would keep me from evil, that I may not cause pain!" So God granted him what he requested. 1 Chronicles 4:10

A The Description of the Jabez "Keep Me from Evil"

1. "Evil" means painful or _____

[5]Then the LORD saw that the wickedness of man was great in the earth, and that every intent of the thoughts of his heart was only evil continually. Genesis 6:5

2. "Keep me" asks that God would act to _____

3. "Pain" means to hurt or experience _____

[6]And the LORD was sorry that He had made man on the earth, and He was grieved in His heart. Genesis 6:6

B The Distinctives of the Jabez "Keep Me from Evil"

1 "Keep me from evil" is not only from suffering but _____

2. "Keep me from evil" is not only from sin but _____

3. "Keep me from evil" is not only for the future but _____

4. "Keep me from evil" is not accomplished by you but _____

5. "Keep me from evil" is not only your pain but _____

II. The Pitfalls of the Jabez "Keep Me from Evil"

A Misconception #1: *God knows my temptations, so praying isn't necessary.*
The prayer to "keep me from evil" greatly affects whether you enter _____

⁴⁰Then He came to the disciples and found them sleeping, and said to Peter, "What? Could you not watch with Me one hour? ⁴¹Watch and pray, lest you enter into temptation. The spirit indeed is willing, but the flesh is weak." Matthew 26:40–41

¹³"And do not lead us into temptation, but deliver us from the evil one." Matthew 6:13a

B Misconception #2: *I don't have to watch out for temptation—I've already prayed!*
The prayer to "keep me from evil" doesn't guarantee that you won't _____

¹²Therefore let him who thinks he stands take heed lest he fall. 1 Corinthians 10:12

C Misconception #3: *I am strong enough to handle temptations.*
The prayer to "keep me from evil" is critically important in _____

¹⁶I say then: Walk in the Spirit, and you shall not fulfill the lust of the flesh. ¹⁷For the flesh lusts against the Spirit, and the Spirit against the flesh; and these are contrary to one another. Galatians 5:16–17a

III. The Principles of the Jabez "Keep Me from Evil"

I have a drawing that shows a Roman gladiator with a very big problem. Somehow, the gladiator has dropped his sword, and he has turned to flee for his life. A hungry lion—claws out, jaws open—is leaping through the air after him. The caption under the drawing reads: *Sometimes you can afford to come in second. Sometimes you can't.* The drawing reminds me how important it is to come in first against temptation. In this contest, there's no second place. The drawing also reminds me of Jabez's unusual plan for winning. *Prayer of Jabez for Teens,* pages 79–80.

A God can keep you during the three types of _____

1. Pray "keep me from evil" due to the temptations of the

¹⁹Now the works of the flesh are evident, which are: adultery, fornication, uncleanness, lewdness, ²⁰idolatry, sorcery, hatred, contentions, jealousies, outbursts of wrath, selfish ambitions, dissensions, heresies, ²¹envy, murders, drunkenness, revelries, and the like. Galatians 5:19–21a

> *A man stood before God, his heart breaking from the pain, sin, and injustice in the world. "Dear God," he cried out, "Look at all the suffering, anguish in your world. Why don't you send help?" God responded, "I did send help. I sent you."*
>
> David J. Wolpe

2. Pray "keep me from evil" due to the temptations of the _____

[15]Do not love the world or the things in the world. If anyone loves the world, the love of the Father is not in him. [16]For all that is in the world—the lust of the flesh, the lust of the eyes, and the pride of life—is not of the Father but is of the world.   1 John 2:15–16

3. Pray "keep me from evil" due to the temptations of the _____

[12]For we do not wrestle against flesh and blood, but against principalities, against powers, against the rulers of the darkness of this age, against spiritual hosts of wickedness in the heavenly places. [13]Therefore take up the whole armor of God, that you may be able to withstand in the evil day, and having done all, to stand.   Ephesians 6:12–13

B **God warns against sin because of the potential** _____

[10]"Now therefore, the sword shall never depart from your house, because you have despised Me, and have taken the wife of Uriah the Hittite to be your wife." [11]Thus says the LORD: "Behold, I will raise up adversity against you from your own house; and I will take your wives before your eyes and give them to your neighbor, and he shall lie with your wives in the sight of this sun. [14]However, because by this deed you have given great occasion to the enemies of the LORD to blaspheme, the child also who is born to you shall surely die."   2 Samuel 12:10–11, 14

C **God works to keep you from evil even during** _____

[13]No temptation has overtaken you except such as is common to man; but God is faithful, who will not allow you to be tempted beyond what you are able, but with the temptation will also make the way of escape, that you may be able to bear it.   1 Corinthians 10:13

Conclusion

[19]Nevertheless the solid foundation of God stands, having this seal: "The Lord knows those who are His," and, "Let everyone who names the name of Christ depart from iniquity." [21]Therefore if anyone cleanses himself from the latter, he will be a vessel for honor, sanctified and useful for the Master, prepared for every good work. [22]Flee also youthful lusts; but pursue righteousness, faith, love, peace with those who call on the Lord out of a pure heart.   2 Timothy 2:19, 21–22

INTERACT WITH JABEZ

1 When Jabez prayed that God would keep him from evil, what do you think he had in mind? List as many different types of evil as you can.

2 Why do you think so few people regularly ask God to keep them from evil? If a person prayed the Jabez Prayer, what specifically would change?

3 What do you think are the three most common sins committed in the lives of Christians today? How do those sins affect God's answers to our prayers for "enlarge my territory" and "put your hand on me"?

4 What is a sin that someone else committed against you or someone close to you that caused great pain? How did that pain affect you?

5 How do you think God ensures that your temptations are never beyond what you are able to bear? If a person deeply believed that to be true, what difference would it make the next time he was tempted?

KEEP ME FROM EVIL!

Wouldn't life be easier without opposition? It would be great to accomplish all our goals and serve God without distractions. But we all know that life will never be that simple. The evil one will try anything to keep you from crossing the finish line of the Jabez journey. He'll throw every impediment in your path in an effort to trip you up.

In this session, you'll find out what the primary temptations you'll face are and how to counter them with godly combat maneuvers, to keep evil from destroying the wonderful work you set out to achieve in God's name.

Top Five Double–Devil–Dupers

1. Tell the devil, "I dare you to cross this line." Put the line on the planet Neptune.

2. Tell the devil you can only be reached by phone. Then get an unlisted number.

3. Tell the devil his home is on fire.

4. Buy a can of that new anti-devil spray called "Get Thee Behind Me!"

5. Let Jesus screen your calls and tell the devil you've stepped out of the office until eternity.

STRANGE BUT TRUE

A lab experiment has been conducted in which a frog is placed in a pan of water. The heat is then raised .0036 of a degree Fahrenheit each second. Two and a half hours later, the frog is dead—without even resisting. The heat has risen so gradually that the frog has actually boiled to death without ever realizing it. How does the devil use this strategy to "burn" you?

CAN YOU TAKE THE HEAT?

Do you have what it takes to withstand temptation? Circle the appropriate answers:

1. I tend to recognize temptation immediately.

   YES   NO

2. I would describe myself as having strong willpower.

   YES   NO

3. I'm not particularly impulsive.

   YES   NO

4. I ask God to keep me from temptation each day.

   YES   NO

5. I have friends and authorities who hold me accountable.

   YES   NO

SCORING: Count each "yes" as 1 point and score yourself this way:

0 – 1	Faulty fire hazard
2	Fairly fire-insulated
3	Favorably fire-resistant
4 – 5	Fully fireproof

KEEP ME FROM EVIL!

Introduction to the Jabez Prayer

¹⁰And Jabez called on the God of Israel saying, "Oh, that You would bless me indeed, and enlarge my territory, that Your hand would be with me, and that You would keep me from evil, that I may not cause pain!" So God granted him what he requested. 1 Chronicles 4:10

I.   The Perspectives on the Jabez "Keep Me from Evil"

A   Pray "keep me from evil" due to the temptation of _____

⁶"God resists the proud, but gives grace to the humble." James 4:6b

²¹So on a set day Herod, arrayed in royal apparel, sat on his throne and gave an oration to them. ²²And the people kept shouting, "The voice of a god and not of a man!" ²³Then immediately an angel of the Lord struck him, because he did not give glory to God. And he was eaten by worms and died. Acts 12:21–23

¹⁰"Hear now, you rebels! Must we bring water for you out of this rock?" Numbers 20:10b

B   Pray "keep me from evil" due to the temptation of _____

⁴²But Jesus called them to Himself and said to them, "You know that those who are considered rulers over the Gentiles lord it over them, and their great ones exercise authority over them. ⁴³Yet it shall not be so among you; but whoever desires to become great among you shall be your servant. ⁴⁴And whoever of you desires to be first shall be slave of all. ⁴⁵For even the Son of Man did not come to be served, but to serve, and to give His life a ransom for many." Mark 10:42–45

C   Pray "keep me from evil" due to the temptation of _____

⁹But those who desire to be rich fall into temptation and a snare, and into many foolish and harmful lusts which drown men in destruction and perdition. ¹⁰For the love of money is a root of all kinds of evil, for which some have strayed from the faith in their greediness, and pierced themselves through with many sorrows. 1 Timothy 6:9–10

D **Pray "keep me from evil" due to the temptation of** _____

⁷And it came to pass after these things that his master's wife cast longing eyes on Joseph, and she said, "Lie with me." ⁸But he refused and said to his master's wife, ⁹"How then can I do this great wickedness, and sin against God?" ¹⁰So it was, as she spoke to Joseph day by day, that he did not heed her, to lie with her or to be with her. ¹¹But it happened about this time, when Joseph went into the house to do his work, and none of the men of the house was inside, ¹²that she caught him by his garment, saying, "Lie with me." But he left his garment in her hand, and fled and ran outside. Genesis 39:7–8a, 9b–12

¹³Now the body is not for sexual immorality but for the Lord, and the Lord for the body. ¹⁸Flee sexual immorality. 1 Corinthians 6:13b, 18a

E **Pray "keep me from evil" due to the temptation of** _____

³³Then He came to Capernaum. And when He was in the house He asked them, "What was it you disputed among yourselves on the road?" ³⁴But they kept silent, for on the road they had disputed among themselves who would be the greatest. Mark 9:33–34

³⁵Then James and John, the sons of Zebedee, came to Him, saying, "Teacher, we want You to do for us whatever we ask." ³⁶And He said to them, "What do you want Me to do for you?" ³⁷They said to Him, "Grant us that we may sit, one on Your right hand and the other on Your left, in Your glory." Mark 10:35–37

²⁴Now there was also a dispute among them, as to which of them should be considered the greatest. Luke 22:24

II. The Practical Steps for the Jabez "Keep Me from Evil"

E _____ **temptations, especially as your territory increases**

V _____ **the sin which so easily ensnares you**

¹Let us lay aside every weight, and the sin which so easily ensnares us, and let us run with endurance the race that is set before us. Hebrews 12:1b

I _____ **the Spirit to fill you with His presence and power**

L _____ **to stand in the power of God's might.**

¹⁰Finally, my brethren, be strong in the Lord and in the power of His might. ¹¹Put on the whole armor of God, that you may be able to stand against the wiles of the devil. ¹⁶Above all, taking the shield of faith with which you will be able to quench all the fiery darts of the wicked one. Ephesians 6:10–11, 16

> *If a man hasn't found something worth dying for, then he isn't fit to live.*
> Martin Luther King

III. The Potential Results from the Jabez "Keep Me from Evil"

A You will become more sensitive to evil and grow in _____

¹⁵But as He who called you is holy, you also be holy in all your conduct, ¹⁶because it is written, "Be holy, for I am holy." 1 Peter 1:15–16

B You will experience that the Lord is able to keep you from _____

²⁴Now to Him who is able to keep you from stumbling, and to present you faultless before the presence of His glory with exceeding joy, ²⁵to God our Savior, Who alone is wise, be glory and majesty, dominion and power, both now and forever. Amen. Jude 1:24–25

C You will not cause pain but joy to others, yourself, and _____

Conclusion

¹In the year that King Uzziah died, I saw the Lord sitting on a throne, high and lifted up, and the train of His robe filled the temple. ²Above it stood seraphim; each one had six wings: with two he covered his face, with two he covered his feet, and with two he flew. ³And one cried to another and said: "Holy, holy, holy is the LORD of hosts; the whole earth is full of His glory!" ⁸I heard the voice of the Lord, saying: "Whom shall I send, and who will go for Us?" Then I said, "Here am I! Send me." Isaiah 6:1–3, 8

INTERACT WITH JABEZ

1   Take a closer look at the five key perspectives (power, possessions, etc.) needing the Jabez protection. List them in the order that you need protection, from the hardest to the easiest for you to face.

2   Of the five perspectives (power, possessions, etc.), which do you think causes more havoc in the lives of people who pray the prayer of Jabez today? Why do you think that?

3   As the Lord enlarges your territory significantly and places His hand on you more fully, how could your temptations change?

4   If a person neglects reading the Bible and praying to the Lord over an extended period of time, do you think he would have a more difficult time with temptations? What about the reverse?

5   Take a few moments to look back through this workbook and write the main lessons that the Lord taught you through this course on the prayer of Jabez.

EXPANDING BORDERS
WITH YOUR JABEZ GROUP

Use these tips for reaching more people through your study sessions.

1

ARE YOU STUDYING JABEZ THROUGH A CHURCH CLASS?

- Call and write each member four, then two weeks, in advance of your sessions. Share your excitement about the breakthrough events that await the group.

- Challenge each group member to bring one friend who needs this life-changing experience. Members might want to present gift copies of *The Prayer of Jabez* to spark interest.

- Write a compelling e-mail about your group, send it to your members, and encourage them to forward it to local friends.

2

ARE YOU STUDYING JABEZ WITH A HOME GROUP?

- Make a special point of building anticipation for your Jabez sessions. Set a goal of 200-percent attendance—all regular members plus one guest apiece.

- Offer copies of the book, *The Prayer of Jabez,* for those who'd like to borrow or buy them.

3

ARE YOU STUDYING JABEZ WITH A LARGER CHURCH GROUP?

- Enlist church leadership to help you promote the sessions and build excitement.

- Thank the pastor for leading the church to the prayer of Jabez and pray the Jabez Prayer for him!

- Consider advertising in local newspapers or on internet event listings.

- Design an attractive flyer giving details about your sessions. Make these available to every church member.

- Appoint "promoters" to use their best people skills to build attendance.

4

NO MATTER HOW YOU'RE STUDYING JABEZ:

- Keep encouraging attendance throughout the sessions. Encourage people not to miss a single meeting.

30 DAYS
THE PRAYER OF JABEZ

Now Jabez was more honorable than his brothers, and his mother called his name Jabez, saying, "Because I bore him in pain." And Jabez called on the God of Israel saying, "Oh, that You would bless me indeed, and enlarge my territory, that Your hand would be with me, and that You would keep me from evil, that I may not cause pain!" So God granted him what he requested.
1 Chronicles 4:9–10

- [ ] DAY ONE
- [ ] DAY TWO
- [ ] DAY THREE
- [ ] DAY FOUR
- [ ] DAY FIVE
- [ ] DAY SIX
- [ ] DAY SEVEN
- [ ] DAY EIGHT
- [ ] DAY NINE
- [ ] DAY TEN
- [ ] DAY ELEVEN
- [ ] DAY TWELVE
- [ ] DAY THIRTEEN
- [ ] DAY FOURTEEN
- [ ] DAY FIFTEEN

- [ ] DAY SIXTEEN
- [ ] DAY SEVENTEEN
- [ ] DAY EIGHTEEN
- [ ] DAY NINETEEN
- [ ] DAY TWENTY
- [ ] DAY TWENTY-ONE
- [ ] DAY TWENTY-TWO
- [ ] DAY TWENTY-THREE
- [ ] DAY TWENTY-FOUR
- [ ] DAY TWENTY-FIVE
- [ ] DAY TWENTY-SIX
- [ ] DAY TWENTY-SEVEN
- [ ] DAY TWENTY-EIGHT
- [ ] DAY TWENTY-NINE
- [ ] DAY THIRTY